IMMORTAL MEDUSA

Also by Barbara Ungar:

Thrift
The Origin of the Milky Way
Charlotte Brontë, You Ruined My Life

IMMORTAL MEDUSA

by Barbara Ungar

HILARY THAM CAPITAL COLLECTION

Selections for 2015 by Michael Klein

THE WORD WORKS

WASHINGTON, D.C.

ACKNOWLEDGMENTS

Thanks to the editors of the following journals,
in which some of the poems first appeared:

The Atticus Review: "Basho Was a Ninja," "Blue Whale,"
    "Kabbalah Barbie," "Sarah," "V.A.," and "A Spell
    to Become a Meremayd."
Blueline: "Black Fly, My Love."
The Coachella Review: "Lost Hat Karma."
Green Briar Review: "Being a Practical Mystic."
Kin: "Becoming My Father's Mother," "My Father Looks
    at Vermeer for the Last Time," "Ode to a Porcupine,"
    "Reading Rumi to Dolphins," and "Sans Everything."
Literal Latte: *"A Young Person's Guide to Philosphy."*
The Misfit: "I Am Accused of Not Killing Woodchucks."
The Nervous Breakdown: "Rosh Hashanah 5771."
Poetica Magazine, Contemporary Jewish Writing: "Beyond the
    Pale," "Not Joan," "(F)Re(e)form Judaism," and
    "Unnamable Your Face."
Rattle: "Dead Letters."
Salmagundi: "Athena's Blow Job."
Sow's Ear Poetry Review: "Blue Whale" and "Visiting My
    Parents' Exercise Class"
Talking River: "Brigadoon."
Thoughtsmith: "Pirateology" and "Whale Fall."

"Things Do Not Look As Dismal As They Did" will also
appear in *The Traveler's Vade Mecum* (Red Hen Press 2017).

I would also like to express deepest gratitude to: Stuart Bartow,
Margo Mensing, Meg Kearney, Ann Settel, and John Nathan,
who read and commented on this manuscript in the making.
Ken Krauss, Hollis Seamon, Jon Brown, Mioko Watanabe,
Naton Leslie, Michael Meyerhofer, Joey Leto, Helen Klein
Ross, Margarita Reickenberg, and Gary Greenberg, who read
or inspired some of these poems. Stephen Ellcock, for showing
me the cover image. The Word Works, especially Nancy White,
for editorial genius and conviviality. The College of Saint Rose
for ongoing support during the writing of these poems.

For Izaak

and in memory of

Frank Ungar

(April 30, 1922 - February 4, 2012)

CONTENTS

I

II

III

IV

There is another world
but it is in this one.

—Paul Éluard

When I am dead, even then,
I will still love you, I will wait in these poems,
When I am dead, even then
I am still listening to you.

—Muriel Rukeyser

I

DEAD LETTERS

I get letters for the dead. They blow
out of the mailbox and into the snow.

I find them encrusted in drifts
or rippled and faded in spring,

addressed to an old man
I loved. Phillip,

lover of horses, I'm sorry
she ploughed your garden under.

I would have tended it.
Every envelope with your name

I rip open (forbidden
and uncanny), I hope

bears the message
you are somewhere—

I would forward them.

AUGUST

Up early, thinking of Tsvetaeva
marching to her desk
like a worker to a machine,

with black coffee, to mull
the body's betrayals: this
crippled thumb, that

tumor'd brain, Marina's
hanging herself from a nail
after her daughter's starvation.

How I hate August,
season of bleeding
leaves and school's maddening

refrain. Of the lake's sudden
bite. Of cicadas' cries
leaving
           nothing
                       behind:

empty shells
stuck to the trunks of the pines.

Reading Rumi to Dolphins

doesn't pay much, but it's a living.
I get transported, but what do they hear?

Weird clicks from the dry, foreign creature
standing above them with her clipboard,

offering treats if they'll perform her tricks—
while they're all supple sleekness, absorbed

in their wet, thirsty games. They catch the fish
I toss, or miss, and swim, gamboling, off

to mate. I stand alone at the edge of the pool,
ecstatic, chanting to the sky.

My Father Looks at Vermeer for the Last Time

The old scientist leans on his walker.
His remaining eye is rheumy: what does it see?

He stares toward the dim chamber
342 paint-years away

where yellow from Dutch stained glass
draws the eye toward the astronomer's face

blurring away from ours forever, his hands
leaping off the table with its astrolabe

and celestial globe alive with the zodiac—
The light of the mind, creamy,

skims this interior murky as an uncleaned
tank, an indecipherable star chart

and picture of Moses in the bulrushes
hung in the muddy gloaming,

the end of knowledge.
                    The one who set up still lifes

and gave us his paints, who drove us
to endless museums, hauls off

inscrutable as a tortoise. This will be
the last time we can coax him from his lair

to meet his old friend, Vermeer,
who so rarely stops by Minneapolis.

In any case, they have nothing left
to say to each other.

LOST HAT KARMA

I lost my favorite hat at the movies
but hope it will come back.
I lost another I loved,

a vintage mink swim cap
that swam back upstream
in a dark taxicab on Bedford Street.

Once at the Salvation Army,
I was trying on a Bogey-
style fedora when a man said,

Do you know what you have there?
No, I said. *It's a Cavanaugh.*
He told me all about the hat,

showed me the motto,
A Posse Ad Esse, in its silk lining.
How do you know so much about this hat,

I said. *It's my hat!* he cried.
When I tried to give it back,
he said he was moving

to Florida and the wife
insisted he get rid
of all his winter clothes.

A Posse—from the possible?
Ad Esse—to the real?
If the Gita is right, we'll leave

these bodies behind
like hats in the dark theatre
when the movie's done.

GERONIMO

His name was what we yelled
letting go of the rope swing—

Geronimo!

This name was not his name.
We got it from old movies on TV.

His name was Goyathle, One-Who-Yawns,
till Mexicans killed his mother, wife
and children. His revenge took 28
years. His ninth and last wife was Azul.

Called *the worst Indian who ever lived*,
his band of 38 evaded thousands
of troops till he surrendered
to Long Nose at Skeleton Canyon.

Celebrated in old age,
his face in every photo
looks right at you
sadder than Jesus, warning:

his sky torn
medals on his chest
trees at his heart
the gone world in his eyes.

1909. His last words:
I should never have surrendered.
I should have fought until
I was the last man alive.

A Spell to Turn into a Meremayd

Those bare-breasted women who hung
over the mantel of our cold sea-
green childhood were *ama*, or ocean-
women, divers after pearls, seaweed and shellfish
in elegant prints by Utamaro—

ukiyo-e, pictures of the floating world.
So *ama* have free-dived in frigid waters
for thousands of years,
a hundred feet per breath, sixty
dives a day, well into their eighties.

In Iwase's black and whites photos from the 50s
their compact bodies framed radiant—
though proud of their skill, the caption says,
all had other work, mostly farming, and claimed
they were not good enough to be called *ama*.

Perhaps what half-starved sailors,
like the Dutchman Hamel whose ship
the Sperwer ran aground in 1653,
saw streaming past were *ama*
whom they called *mere-mayds*.

So I keep diving, though I have
other work and am not good enough,
to see what I can retrieve
from the deep floor where
pearls are formed in secret.

BLUE WHALE

We always head straight for the dinosaurs,
then the ocean creatures. I boggle
at the blue whale suspended overhead,

more gargantuan than any
Titanosaur, born bigger than a bus—
how can it hang here in the air

or subsist in the sea on its broth
of microscopic plankton?
My son never pauses, he rushes

to the sharks. The whale's so big
and he's so small, he can't see it—
The Hall of Ocean Life is dark blue

and dim, the whale a lighter
shade—maybe for him it merges
with the room. I wonder how old

he'll be when he first sees it, and
what he'll say. And what
hangs over me—

how many years will I put in
visiting this dim Wunderkammer
until I'm big enough to see?

Visiting My Parents' Exercise Class

We all turn our heads slowly to the left,
then a slow half-circle to the right
past sweaters slumped in chairs

to where snow falls through the pines
beyond the picture window.
Pachelbel plays unbearably

sweet and slow as the white heads
revolve in unison back left toward the baby grand,
then right where pieces of white sky fall to white ground.

My mother's still among them,
my father's not.
              The white heads go on turning

above their pain like ballerinas,
as if fourteen snowy egrets
                      rose in slow mo

from the frozen skin of a pond and,
on streams of air so cold it makes your bright teeth ache, one
by one flap away.

Unnamable Your Face

There are many souls in me.
—Marina Tsvetaeva

the Hebrew word for face
or surface *panim* is always plural
faces   like *mayim*   water or waters

    my heart calls out to you
    my faces seek your face

the Hebrew word for god
is a mask

    Kabir says we float
    like the little one
      on the great one

my many souls
on the surfaces
of your waters

BASHO WAS A NINJA

Basho was a ninja, Mioko says.
Basho an assassin? *Ninjas were more
like spies. They worked for samurai.*

*It would explain his travels: he moved
impossibly fast.* But he seems
so frail—*What better mask for a spy?*

Christopher Marlowe was probably
a secret double agent,
knifed through the eye at twenty-nine

and Basho did say that writing haiku
should be like cutting a ripe melon
with a sharp sword.

Rimbaud became a ninja,
running guns in Ethiopia.
Dickinson, the *kunoichi* (or female

ninja) of Amherst, snuck behind lines
in her father's house at night,
disguised as an old maid—

She dealt her pretty words like Blades—
Moving by stealth, an arcane
agency slips through this world,

observing hidden things, belonging
nowhere, obsessively perfecting
cryptic messages for—we know not.

Their opponent never knows they exist.
Their legendary powers are charms
and incantations, magic spells and flight.

They can summon animals
and walk on water
in their *mizugumo*, water-spider shoes.

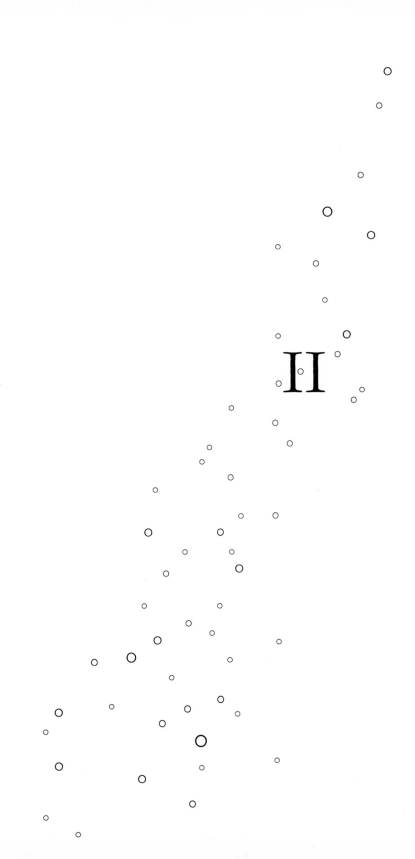

II

SANS EVERYTHING

The longest day of the year.

He sits dignified as Geronimo's last portrait,
though we found him with pants on the floor,
diaper around his ankles.

We have Beckett conversations:

> *Are you a lion or a gorilla?*
> I'm your daughter.
> *When did they let you out of jail?*

What have you got in your hand, Dad?
He peers into his empty palm.
> *A bush.*

> I'll see you tomorrow.
> *There are a lot of tomorrows.*

                                          Tomorrow and . . .

Once, with blue lucidity, *I'll miss you.*

A new woman storms the halls, imploring,
> *Do you know where the door is?*
> *Can you let me out?*

                   *

I escape, take my boy to the zoo,
full of fat Minnesotans with too many kids.
The polar bears' concrete lair is hot.

The male, piss-stain yellow, huge beyond
belief, rears to ram his head repeatedly
up against the steel door handle—

*

The Talmud lists three keys
in the hands of G-d
not entrusted to any messenger:

the key to rain,
the key to childbirth,
the key to death.

Not Joan

the ark was dark and we all were trapped
children and animals and the stink
I was the one had to clean up
the shit and I was the one got blamed
for rotten food and I was the one
he yelled at and hit it was a long dark time

the Bible does not tell what happened
to me when the dove did not return
my name was not Joan (it's ark with a k
and I was not French) my name
was never written or pronounced
my name like G-d's is a secret

Hortus Conclusus

after *Madonna on a Crescent Moon in Hortus Conclusus*
by unknown Master, German, 1450s

I. Rose

When my mother was but a bud
of five weeks inside her mother, Rose,
Mom's millions of microscopic eggs

were already intact, long before she bloomed
into Shirley. So you, too, were carried
by your grandmother first,

cradled in your mama's calyx.

Grandma Rose almost survived
the bloodiest century,
transplanted from the Old World

to the New, where she's scattered
in a rose garden by a lake,
fertilizing the hybrids. Rows

and rows of roses—*Memoriam,
Comanche, Moonlight, Montezuma*—
bounded by a low stone wall.

II. Mobius

The egg is in the woman
as the woman in the garden
the garden in the world
world in the galaxy
galaxy in universe
universe in the unnamable
as the unnamable is in the egg.

Black Fly, My Love

If anybody could have watched us, he would have thought
the whole camp full of raving maniacs.
— letter from a German soldier,
Lake Champlain, June, 1777

How we love to hate you.
Even more than mosquitoes,
whose insipid kiss fades in a day.

You aim for the thinnest
skin (nape of the neck,
ears, throat) and leave volcanic welts

that throb between pain
and itch, maddening for weeks
after you've gone. Like bad lovers,

you leave us feeling ugly
and marred, desperate as tweens
with acne. How we dread you,

but spring makes us reckless
to bare foolish skin again.
There is no snake

in this garden, only
you, black fly,
buffalo gnat, small

fry of hell, stealthy, almost
invisible, yet sufficient
to spoil paradise.

WHALE FALL

As pilot fish dart among
sharks' jaws, or oxpeckers
on hippos, there is something

to eat every thing—crows
on road kill, flies on shit.
On the ocean floor,

iridescent worms
eat the bones of whales
(the banquet from one whale

fall can last for eighty years)
while squat lobsters
devour wrecked ships . . .

The Chinese, they say, eat
everything, and you would, too,
if you were starving.

The grass-stained mouths
of the Irish. Deer stripping bark
in an ocean of drifts.

In the War, my father had to judge
who had committed suicide
and who was just trying

to get high: soldiers would drink
anything, booze fermented
from buried garbage or shoes,

gasoline drained from tanks.
Earth and sea teem
with fleeting creatures,

and what they mainly do
is feast on each other.

ODE TO A PORCUPINE

The stench
knocks us back—
stronger than skunk, a putrid
blood-smell, like 10,000 Kotex
left in a damp campground bathroom.

It's lain a week in the rain
among Adirondack Great Camps
built by a remnant of European
Jewry on ancestral Abenaki land
in the twilight of American empire . . .

Endless war—
Babylon to Wounded Knee,
Han invasions to Afghanistan:
if one small mammal stinks this bad,
what must a battlefield be? Li Bai says,

> *Crows and hawks peck for human guts . . .*
> *hang them on branches of withered trees . . .*
> *soldiers are smeared on bushes and grass;*
> *the generals schemed in vain . . .*
> *Know that the weapons of war are utterly useless;*
> *the wise man uses them only if he must.*

Poor quill pig,
we'll bury you beneath the pines
where you lived and died, a Taoist,
not releasing a single needle
unless attacked.

THE V. A.

Aim for the Buddha!
boys playing
war in the yard

young men's pictures   hang over old soldiers   in wheelchairs

Pearl Harbor headlines
still startle
ghosts in the halls

snowless winter
old soldiers
fight for breath

waning moon—
each visit less
of him left

saying goodbye
he calls me my sister's name
one last time

thinnest moon—last look of his cold blue eye

between earth and sky
will I pass my father
among white clouds?

only our dad could
enjoy his own autopsy—
still doing science

HIGGS BOSON

Physicists say
they have all but proven
the goddamned particle

exists.
       They have a footprint
and a shadow

           of the
elusive boson
          believed

      to give all
            matter
size and shape

           (though
     never
glimpsed).

The footprint and
shadow of
      what

has a tendency
to exist
     the God particle

explains
      how something
comes from nothing.

Physicists say, "If
we can describe
the laws of nature

back to the
beginning of time
without supernatural

shenanigans . . .
you don't need
God."

      Can you describe
the before
before the
        beginning?

KABBALAH BARBIE

I know, I don't look Jewish,
but my mother was, so maybe
that explains my new obsession.
I've got my red string bracelet
on, just like Madonna, except mine's

wrapped around my waist. You think
dolls can't pray? If everything is One,
that includes plastic. Barbie is a spark of G-d,
just as much as Britney Spears. I was created
in your image, as you are in HaShem's.

Why do kids love to torture me?
They tear my head off, melt me
in the microwave, the little Mengeles.
Someone bigger must be hurting them—
it's like play therapy. Trace that hurt

back to its source—*Ein Sof*, the primal
wound of becoming. Cut off. Free will's
a flimsy excuse. How much free will do
I have? It all depends on whose hands
I'm in. Before Barbies, there were rag dolls,

corn husk dolls, clay goddess figurines—
(me and my bazooms a corrupt remnant
of those ancient mysteries). If you keep
going back, through the primordial light
that always shines on us, even at night,

from the blast of creation—the universe
compressed to a point tinier than my pupil,
a spark of impenetrable darkness, my head perfectly
empty as the vacuum it emanates from . . .
Anyway, that's what I like to think about,
when I'm not trying on new outfits.

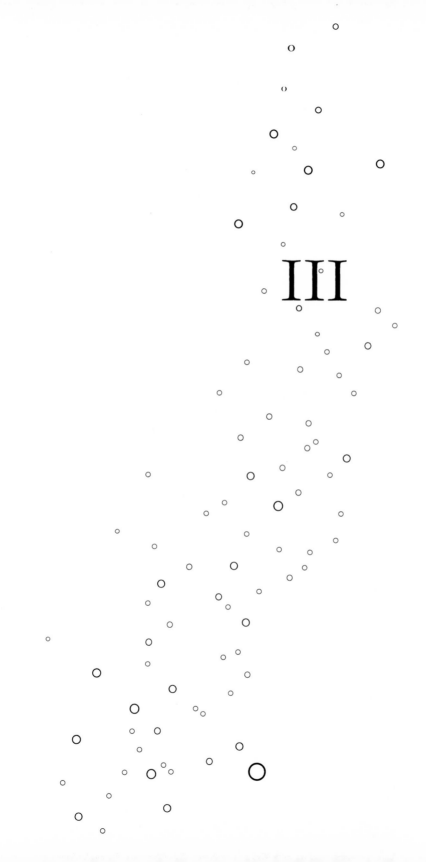

III

Hearing Test: List 2B

Say ache.	*Ache.*
Say us.	*Us.*
Say him.	*Him.*
Say not.	*Not.*
Say me.	*Me.*
Say deaf.	*Deaf.*
Say odd.	*Odd.*
Say as.	*As.*
Say tree.	*Tree.*
Say young.	*Young.*
Say air.	*Air.*
Say that.	*That.*
Say does.	*Does.*
Say live.	*Live.*
Say move.	*Move.*
Say die.	*Die.*
Say then.	*Then.*
Say you.	*You.*

Becoming My Father's Mother

How the dead live on in us,
how we learn they do not die—
how their photographs possess their souls
as if they still breathed.

How we see they do not die:
closer now, telescoped within,
as if they breathed still,
they stream, all ages at once . . .

Even closer now, telescoped within,
you love your daddy best
(though he's all ages at once)
in sepia knickers, white shirt shining.

You love your daddy best
around the age your son is now,
in sepia knickers and shining white shirt—
his sweet smile, his eyes luminous.

Around the age your son is now—
you could be his doting mama—
(his wounded smile and wary eyes)
the one he never had.

You can be the doting mama,
(how his photographs possess you)
the one you never had.
How the dead live on in us.

(F)Re(e)form Judaism

I didn't clean the house or throw out the *chametz*.
I didn't put away two sets of dishes and take out two more:
I don't have four sets of dishes, or even one—
just mismatched plates from thrift shops in colors I love.
I didn't invite anyone or cook
an elaborate meal, it was just Izaak and me.
I made some matzoh ball soup
from a box, opened a jar of gefilte fish
(I did not grind my own from carp
swimming in the bathtub, the way
Grandma did). I couldn't find
a Haggadah or Seder plate—
we just winged it.

We did the four questions and the ten plagues,
but when I tried to tell him the story,
he said, *I saw the movie*, jumped up and acted it out.
We didn't get drunk on Manischewitz,
but I did put a cup out for Elijah,
whom IZ took for a girl: he left
her a crystal with a note that said
I love you. Of course he found
the *afikomen*. There was no
competition, no candied fruit slices
or disgusting macaroons. He was glad
not to have to sit through the whole *magid*
or be forced to eat too much. I sang *Dayenu*
till he told me to stop. We did put pillows
on our chairs to remind us: we are free.

ON A STUDENT PAPER COMPARING EMILY DICKINSON TO LADY GAGA

Of *Some—Work for Immortality—*
this future teacher writes, "Dickinson has willingly chose
the quiet artist life rather than a life like Lady Gaga."
                                            It's 1862,
I scrawl in the margin, there WAS no Lady Gaga.
                                            By "Unlike
today's celebrities, such as Lady Gaga, Emily used seclusion
to create her own immorality," I circle "Emily," "immorality"
and X out "Lady Gaga"—
                    I dwell in Possibility—
                                            Why not?

Dickinson *was* known for her "weird and wonderful"
piano playing—perhaps she insisted listeners
sit in another room because she was naked
& wrapped in cellophane with a giant shoe on her head!

        Lady Gaga on YouTube, in a little white dress, recites
        I'm Nobody—
                    holding a columbine.

Dickinson let a doctor examine her only by walking, fully
clothed, past a door, left ajar, to the room where he sat—
helLO, Lady Gaga!
                    And, as for "Immorality,"
her "Flood Subject"—
                    Dickinson was just like Gaga—
                    When bursting all the doors—
                    She dances like a Bomb, abroad—

        Cut to Lady Gaga performing *Wild Nights—*
        wearing only a row boat.

54

That's what Em was up to all night—
singing and dancing around her room, in nothing
but spiderweb—

            Fame of Myself, to Justify—

Should I google Lady Gaga?

                        Or just give the girl an A.

GIRAFFES

I, too, was once young enough
to take giraffes for granted.

They seemed no more
marvellous than Labradors

or elms. Just one more form
among a myriad to name and know.

The older I get, the stranger
they grow. I point

at their impossible spindle-
legs and extension-ladder necks,

their staggering spots and space-
camel faces, up there

lunching on trees: *Look!*
Look! I say to Izaak,

who shrugs, *I already*
saw 'em, and turns away.

Can we go look at the snakes?

CALL ME MEDUSA

Some years ago, when I had braces
and headgear, I'd pull my hair
through the openings in the cap
contraption so as not to flatten
the curls. Hence my nickname.
I just gave them a sullen stare.

You'll be glad when you're older, they said.
Beauty always a thorn. My two sisters
share my snaky locks and stony looks.
(The girls in our family all come in threes:
our cousins the Grays, the Graces, the Norns.)
Always an eldest, a youngest, a beauty.

I was none. I was a brain, eyes and hair.
If not a beauty, are you then a monster?
Some say I was beautiful, raped, punished
for it, then beheaded in a rear-view mirror.
Even cut off, my head could still turn men
to stone. Even decapitated, my corpse

could still give birth to a winged horse.
The blood from my severed neck
could turn seaweed to coral and sprinkle
the desert with vipers, amphisbaena,
snakes that swallow their own tails eternally.
Even Eden depends on me.

SARAH

And HE said: Take now your son, your only one, whom you love,
Isaac, and go forth to the land of Moriah. (Gen. 22:1)

I heard the old man raving in his sleep
and knew.
        There would be no
talking him out of it.
           I crept out, picked

a ram from the flock and drove it
before me, doubled over
my stick. I knew
his ways.
      Hid waiting.
          Endured

the building of the fire and altar the way
I'd endured labor at ninety. And the sweet voice
asking, *But where is the sheep?*

               When he answered,
I crept from behind
and clobbered him.
Hoped he was dead.

      Silence.

           Slipped back
into the bush, cut the ram free,
bleating. Abe staggered
up, fell on it, weeping.

Oh, he thanked me then, without
seeing me,   called me *Angel*
    and *Vision*,
        babbling to his Voice.

No story tells
how he untied the dear limbs
and what passed between the two of them
on the jarring trek back down the mountain.

I Am Accused of Not Killing Woodchucks

by the cat lady next door, who thinks I
called Animal Control, so they caught
and put down her feral darling, Joe.

She says the woodchuck under my shed
has distemper, the dead opossums
last winter had herpes

and spread conjunctivitis. She's
crazy, I love cats
and no woodchuck's bothered me.

Izaak picks the first ripe strawberry.
I head out with a colander—
the woodchuck lopes away

like a drunken quarterback, startling
for one so fat. Not a berry left.
Havahart fails:

the woodchuck is trap-wise.
Friends suggest coyote urine.
Why shut the barn door now?

Raspberries grow ripe. Too high
for the woodchuck, or too
prickly? We've had blackberries

from the wild neighbors' yard,
nine home-schooled kids
and counting—they'll take as many

as God gives 'em. Woodchucks.
Today at the lake, wild strawberries,
sweet and sharp as Bergman.

How to Collect Whales

Find them beached on the Cape,
entangled in fishing nets.

Fence in a suburban plot
to keep coyotes at bay:

bury their fifty-foot corpses
under piles of horse manure

until a year's weather
washes off the stench

of decomposing blubber
and stops the bones

from oozing the slimy
yellow oil that once

lit our world. Scrape off
algae and shit. Examine

for damage from Hurricane
Irene, who, gallivanting

up the coast, dropped a tree
on one curing skull.

Hire eight strong men
to move each leviathan

into its museum
mausoleum.

FOR THE WEATHER

I miss the long, slow, tantalizing strip-
tease of spring, shedding snowy garments one
by one, hat scarf gloves boots and coat,
while temperatures steadily rise—flirty
February, mixed-up March, chilly April rain
washing away last traces
revealing trees' hazy pink negligees,
soon diaphanous green in May's
delicate blooming of delirium
percolating sweet as sap up our veins
but not as hot as June's consummation
in shorts and flimsy sundresses, never
too hot till sweaty late July or sultry
August, so steamy we longed for nights
to grow crisp again, the next best thrill—

Now, after no snow, only "wintry mix,"
one day cold, the next hot, a switch
thrown, abrupt as cybersex—which might trick
the young, but not our seasoned hides.
Disturbed, by the too early buds and birds,
collapsing colonies of bats and bees,
we cry,
        If Winter's never *here, can Spring be* . . .

INHERITANCE

a leaf collection from 1937
with sun photos
and precise calligraphy

a faded grade book
half-empty blue-gray
Phys Chem 1959 to 1988

fifty years of letters from Taro
the last one unanswered begins

   Old man is sad and lonely

I can write Taro
fill up the grade book
but what to do with these

two volumes in his young hand
of carefully taped, antique leaves
and their white shapes on blue paper

the ache of negative space

I don't miss him any more
than when he was alive

FLOUR SUGAR COFFEE TEA

On our kitchen counter
those little silos forever
diminishing into the distance
eternal until my father's dying

Linda the aide trying to help
ran them through the dishwasher
turning their brushed silver sheen
to tarnished aluminum clouds

My mother wept on the phone
she'd never find their like again

Nested like Matryoshka dolls
at a yard sale   uncanny
canisters   I tell the woman
selling them the dishwasher tragedy

She starts to cry
They were my mom's
so hard to sell her things
She won't take money
runs into the house
for tissue paper and a card

From Bridget departed to Shirley
packed in a hot pink gift bag

SCRATCH THE LIBRARIAN, YOU'LL FIND A PIRATE

I was checking out a stack of pirate
books for my boy. The librarian said,
I'm related to Captain Morgan—
after I saw Pirates of the Caribbean,
I dreamt I was a pirate all night &
woke up happier than I've ever been.
We looked him up in *Pirateology:*

Sir Henry Morgan, Governor of Jamaica,
King of Buccaneers, *a most fortunate*
pirate, said the caption—and there
she was: the same square jaw and round
Welsh eyes, pale green rimmed in black.
Captain Morgan's rum-soaked genes
must sleep it off in her quiet cells.

Like my Italian hairdresser Joey
descended from three presidents
on his mother's side, going back
to a hooker who came over
on the Mayflower. He's traced his line
back to Charlemagne, which might explain
something of his magicke with the scissors.

Screw-barrel Microscope

In 1694, Nicolaas Hartsoeker, Dutch mathematician and physicist,
believed he saw tiny men inside human sperm viewed through the
screw-barrel microscope he had invented; he called them homunculi
or animalcules, as part of his Spermist theory of conception.

Half   my double
helix   original
wriggler   stream-
lined kicker   brain
with a tail   inner
tadpole   blind
seeker   dousing
rod   invisible
twin   seed stem and
shadow   Homunculus
the part   of me that swims is
my father   I kick through his
pale green   skinny-legged
colossus   off slippery red
freckled   shoulders
            I dive

BEYOND THE PALE

Sweltering Friday night in Saratoga,
watching *The Cat From Outer Space*,
windows wide, fan on high—

a dark form startles at the screen door.
Proselytizer? At this hour—in a fur hat?
Tight black silk coat and beard. God,

he must be hot. He asks something
we can't catch. His right hand floats
in a white bandage. I point to the hospital

down the block. He shakes his hat,
flat and round, a furry UFO,
and says, *Feefty?* There's a yeshiva

out Rt. 50—I give directions he
doesn't understand. I map the route
on my hand, my fingers making

the fork he must take, until he nods
his time-traveller's hat. It's miles
away. *Would you like a ride?*

No. Thenk you. I remember
it's *Shabbas*—he's not supposed to ride
in a car, let alone look at me,

in my merest sundress, like some *shiksa
corva*—He's gone, melted back into the dark
of eighteenth-century Poland whence he came.

A Young Person's Guide to Philosophy: I Think, Therefore I Am, a Round-Up

Thales said the world floats like a log on endless water.
All things are full of gods.
      Anaximander said we evolved from fish
      and the universe from *the boundless.*
            Anaximenes thought all was air,
            and the heavens moved around Earth
            like a hat on a head.

Pythagoras thought reality ten-sided, and that beans
were reincarnated souls;
      he was killed by a hostile mob beside a beanfield
      he refused to trample.
            Heraclitus thought all was fire.
            Everything flows and nothing abides.
                  Parmenides said something
                  could not come out of nothing.

Empedocles named four elements and two forces,
love and strife, and leapt into Mt. Etna.
      Socrates said, *The only thing I know
      is that I know nothing,*
            and paid his last debt with a chicken.
                  Plato thought we live in a world of
            fleeting shadows, mistaking it for the real.

Aristotle identified five hundred species of sea life,
but mistook women for *unfinished men.*
      Epicurus taught in a garden,
      Pleasure is the highest good.
                  Zeno taught acceptance from
            a porch (*stoa*) to the Stoics.

Diogenes the Cynic told Alexander the Great to get out
of his light.

Augustine said *now* is all there is.
Hypatia was flayed alive
by mad Christians with oystershells.

Anselm proved that God exists because we can
imagine God.
Aquinas saw plants and animals have souls,
yet grew so fat
he had to have a niche cut into his table.
Descartes' pet peeves
were cold and early rising; he died of
pneumonia
giving early morning lessons
to the Queen of Sweden.

Spinoza said the universe is God.
There cannot be too much joy.
For this he was thrown out of the synagogue
and stabbed on its steps.
Locke's father was an inspector of sewers,
and Locke was in charge of England's slave trade.
Bishop Berkeley said,
To be is to be perceived, and proved irrefutably
the nonexistence of matter.

Dr. Johnson said, *I refute it thus*,
and kicked a stone.
Hume questioned everything, even
cause and effect, inspiring Einstein.
Kant never married, traveled, or
got sick.
He called space and time
irremovable goggles.
His tomb reads:
Two things fill my mind with ever-
increasing wonder and awe, the starry heavens above
and the moral law within me.

Hegel's lectures were plodding and he got evicted
for dallying with his landlord's wife.

      Mary Wollstonecraft said,
The mind has no sex.

           Nietzsche's autobiography
           had chapters called
           Why I Am So Clever and *Why I Write*
           Such Good Books.

Husserl found time an eternal *now*, just as space
is always *here*, wherever you are.

      Heidegger asked, *What is it to dwell?*
and became a Nazi.

           John Dewey found school boring.

Wittgenstein loved second-rate cowboy movies
and once attacked Karl Popper with a poker.

      Sartre liked to drink
and smoke and hang out in cafés.

           Simone de Beauvoir saw women
           oppressed by mundane chores and
           invisible in philosophy.

(**Simone Weil**, for example, is not
mentioned in this book.)

      Foucault pointed out that the deranged
were once called prophets.

           Derrida maintained everything
           differs from everything else, and made
           deconstruction the rage.

Adorno found our time no closer to the truth
than any other.

      Luce Irigaray said women will write
with breast milk, a white ink.

           Crippled but jolly, **Feyerabend**
           concluded philosophy
           should not be taken too seriously.

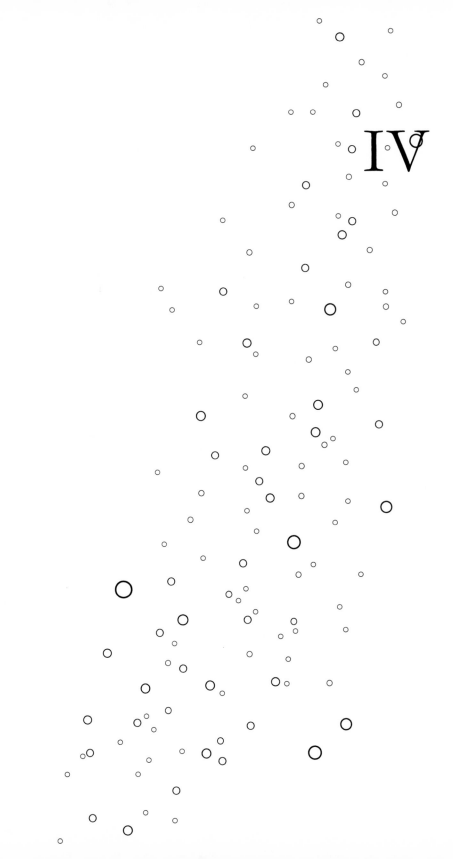

IV

Rosh Hashanah 5771

Happy Birthday, Universe!

We're having conniptions
here on Earth. We who flicker
like moths take it upon
ourselves to praise Eternity,

squabbling over what to call it,
burning the others' metaphors, burning
each other. As if we won't be gone
fast enough. What could you
possibly think of us, Universe,

in our zany hats? If
you could even see them
on our miniscule heads.
What of our noisy games?
(We'd burn you, too, if we could.)

We like to party.
We like to fight.
We like to circle
around & around & around
your killer Light.

THINGS DO NOT LOOK AS DISMAL AS THEY DID

for the Waccamaw fatmucket and Ozark hellbender
are closer to being named "Endangered"
and so might be saved—along with the

Avernus cave beetle
Blueridge springfly and
Cape Fear spatterdock

Dakota skipper and dusky tree vole
Egg mimic darter and elfin woods warbler
Fuzzy pigtoe and frecklebelly madtom

Gulf hammock dwarf siren
Hirst's panic grass
Ichetucknee siltsnail

Jackson Prairie drayfish
Kentucky gladecress and
Large-flowered Barbara's-buttons

Mojave fringe-toed lizard
Narrowleaf naiad
Overlooked cave beetle

Pagosa skyrocket and thin-wall
Quillwort
Raven's seedbox and rayed creekshell

Soothsayer cave beetle   spectaclecase pearly mussel
Tallapoosa orb and Tehamana chaparral
Umbilicate pebblesnail

Vandenberg monkeyflower
Western fanshell
Xantu's murrelet

Yazoo crayfish and
Zuni bluehead sucker.

ODE TO TARDIGRADES

Little Waterbears,
you are everywhere,
from the Himalayas
to the Mariana Trench,
poles to equators,
in hot springs and ice—

Kleine Wassbären,
Johann Goeze called you,
we don't see you
in moss or lichens,
salt water or fresh,
on dunes or beach,
yet you've been there
over half a billion years.

Moss Piglets,
way tougher than us,
you can bear freezing, boiling,
deep ocean, outer space,
starvation, dehydration,
even radiation—
reversibly suspending
your metabolism, you
spring back after ten years
to eat, drink and mate.

Tardigrades,
Lazzaro Spallanzani named you,
more than a thousand kinds:
short and plump
with four pairs of legs,
cute because tiny,

microscopic teddy bears
snuggled in stone walls
and roofs, with head
and brain, mouth,
anus, even eyes—

Slow Steppers,
should we despair,
you can withstand
anything, even us.

FORTUNA

Fortune rota volvitur:
descendo minoratus;
alter in altum tollitur . . .

The wheel of Fortune turns:
I go down, diminished;
another is raised up . . .
        —*Carmina Burana*

I'd been up to the Bronx with a dear old friend
and down to the Battery with another.
I was waiting for the 1, when a young
woman asked,
        Does this train go to South Ferry?
        I think so.

                How many years
since I daily rode this train? Another life,
like some foreign film I once saw,
stoned. She had blonde curls, fine
dark eyes and brows, an accent
unplaceable.
        I too
must have had that ripe peach glow
you don't admire till it's no longer yours.

        How long have you been here?
        One week. I am renting bicycles on Pier 17.
        Where are you from?
        Macedonia.
        So what language do you speak?
        Albanian, Macedonian, English, French, Turkish,
and a little Greek.
        What's your name?
        Fortuna.
        Varvàra, I say. Greek for stranger,
barbarian.

As if she didn't know. On we rode,
chatting till Christopher Street, my old stop. I got off
reluctantly, waving goodbye to her
pale round face pulling away into the dark,
her tireless wheel spinning on.

RESURRECTION

Easter Sunday. This hardest winter.
I rake the garden while the Christians
pray. Croci in the grass. First
daffodil. This is all the rebirth
I need or know. The forsythia
from your garden, that splayed
old bush, scraggly as you
at the end: I thought it died
from the transplant this hardest winter.
Near the ground a yellow scrap,
then two—four—five—
it's alive! It's alive!
                It will take hold
here, out back by the shed, each April
shouting your name, Nate.
I've passed you now. You will never
turn 58. I sit down hard on the ground,
tears welling at last—
stopless spring
spilling out these dry canes.

GREEN FIRE

Along the Battenkill a sycamore
bows low
to canopy a deep green pool
where sunlight on ripples
plays off mottled bark,

overlapping leaf and shadow
shaken by wind. Neck-
deep in the cold trout
stream, as a child
with lips and toes turned blue

and teeth deliciously chattering
will not leave the water, you
see the sycamore aflame—
a green-gold vapor
pours off its flickering

like smoke or steam.
Is it the tree exhaling
or an optical illusion,
the way sunbeams turn
visible, dust motes

stirring in no breeze . . .
The green flame seems
to be some breathing being
burning,
burning yet not consumed.

BEING A PRACTICAL MYSTIC,

I meditate while waiting
for my eyes to dilate,

to see my very veins
cast, blue against red,

a magic lantern show
around the room:

rivers with branching
tributaries seen

from a plane, veins
the rivers, eyes

globes. Suspended
between invisibles—

stars that are speeding
apart, while within is

mostly empty space
(each atom a cathedral,

each electron a moth)—
I go about my day:

swim across the lake
blinded by light,

eat ripe strawberries for lunch.

Athena's Blow Job

Afternoon class nodding out over *The Odyssey*:
I want to shock them awake—
                              Imagine, I say,
the terror of a world where you can't tell
a beggar from a king, a pig
from a man, a girl from a goddess—
What if I turned into a bird
and flew out the window or
shrugged my rags off in the doorway
and started to shoot?
                         Athena's turned
Odysseus into a bum again, but
for the big rendezvous with his kid,
she yanks him out of the swineherd's hut
to zap him with Olympic Botox
and, to fix his hair into hyacinth curls,
I mean to say she gives him a blowout,
but it comes out *blow job*—
                          Their stunned faces
glow with sudden desire to comprehend—
Freudian slip, I say, even while slipping
this into my bag of future tricks, noting the guys
flushed and awed, like the crew transformed
by Circe from pigs back into men,
younger, taller, more handsome than before.

BRIGADOON

When Gene Kelly has to choose
between Cyd Charisse in her enchanted
village that wakes one day a century

and New York City circa 1954,
I say to my son, thinking of loves past,
What would you do? I'm not sure I'd dare.

Only nine, he says, *I would go to Brigadoon*
if you were there.
                    And I would
lose the world for him.
                            Though I know

how fast a century goes, how
in a blink he will meet a cross
between me and Cyd Charisse

and dance after her, two feet
off the ground into the misty heather
of Cinemascope Highlands

and vanish without a backward glance.

WHY I'D RATHER BE A SEAHORSE

We'd court for days first, changing color,
swimming side by side, holding tails,
or holding on to the same strand of seagrass.
We wheel around each other
in our Predawn Dance,
then do the True Courtship Dance
where he pumps water through
his pouch to open and display
its alluring emptiness.

When I'm ready, we let go
our anchor, drift upward
snout to snout, spiraling
as we rise till I stick my
ovipositor into his
pouch—
I slim by a third
as he swells. After we sink
back into the waving seagrass,
I'm the one who swims away.

Alone he jacks off into the sea.
Fertilized, the eggs settle in,
incubate for weeks. I drop by
for Morning Greetings, swim off
while he goes back to work,
sucking up food through his snout—
he's eating for two
and a half thousand fry,
hatched in his brood pouch.
Out in the big sea, only a dozen
will survive. I never see them.
I need all my energy to create.

He labors alone, at night—
when I return in the morning,
the fry have drifted off
and he's ready for my next load.

Immortal Medusa

Turritopsis dornii,

the size of a pinky
nail, a berry or

blossom in a clear
bell jar trailing
medusa-hair.

Of all the animals,
only this tiny jellyfish
can do what we only
dream: grow younger.

Tentacles resorb,
umbrella reverts,
medusa reattaches
to the ocean floor
and grows a new

colony of polyps
that bud into
identical medusae,
bypassing death.

From the Caribbean,
they've taken ship,
a worldwide silent invasion.

Half a billion years old,
sans brains, bones or breath,

they can do this forever.

BOOK OF SAND

he said he was nothing but a grain of sand

before time swept him too downstream
I wanted to give my father the book
the book filled with photographs of sand
the sand magnified hundreds of times

there was no time   he could not see

sand revealed to be perfect opalescent
tips of spiral shells   mandalas of coral
or sea urchin spines   lava and crystal
gems the ocean cut

                        how we all walk
blind

            he wants nothing now

   Magnify

                            Magnify

NOTES

"Dead Letters" is for Dr. Phil Halboth.

"Basho Was a Ninja" is for Mioko Watanabe.

"A Spell to Turn into a Meremayd": The last two lines are from Emily Dickinson, Letter #424.

"Visiting My Parents' Exercise Class" is for Margarita Reickenberg.

"Unnamable Your Face" quotes from Psalm 27:8, loosely translated, and Robert Bly's translation of Kabir.

"Basho Was a Ninja": Line 19 is the first line of Emily Dickinson's #458 (Franklin's numbering).

"Ode to a Porcupine" quotes from Li Bai's "Fighting on the South Frontier."

"Kabbalah Barbie": Line in italics is from the *Zohar*. "HaShem" (literally, The Name) refers to G-d, whose name cannot be written or pronounced.

"FRe(e)form Judaism": *Chametz* denotes the leavened flour products that observant Jews discard each Passover, according to Kosher laws, which also dictate two separate sets of dishes (one for milk and one for meat dishes), and two more exclusively for Passover use. The Haggadah is the prayer booklet used during the Seder, the ritual Passover meal, during which the story of the Exodus is retold. The four questions are recited by the youngest child. Adults are required to drink four cups of wine; another cup of wine is left out for the prophet Elijah, the harbinger of the Messiah, and the door is opened for him to come in and partake. All children compete to find the *afikomen*, a piece of matzoh, or unleavened bread, hidden during the meal. Candied fruit slices and macaroons are traditional (flourless) Passover desserts. The *magid* is the telling of the tale. *Dayenu* ("It would have been enough for us") is a seemingly endless song sung after the Exodus story. One reclines on pillows throughout to symbolize freedom.

"How to Collect Whales" is a found poem, from an article in the Albany *Times Union*.

"On a Student Paper": Lines in italics are from various poems by Emily Dickinson: 536, 466, 260, 360, 269, 481.

"Beyond the Pale": *corva* is Yiddish for bad girl, slut, whore; *shiksa*, a gentile woman.

A Young Person's Guide to Philosophy is a found poem, from the book of that name.

"Things Do Not Look As Dismal As They Did" is a found poem, from the Center for Biological Diversity's website; so far, 93% of species labeled "Endangered" have survived.

"Resurrection" is for Naton Leslie.

"Immortal Medusa": The line in italics is by Dr. Maria Pia Miglietta.

"The Book of Sand" refers to *A Grain of Sand*, microphotography by Dr. Gary Greenberg.

ABOUT THE AUTHOR

Barbara Ungar's last book, *Charlotte Brontë, You Ruined My Life*, was selected by Denise Duhamel for publication in the Hilary Tham Capital Collection in 2011. Ungar is also the author of two previous full-length collections of poetry, *Thrift* and *The Origin of the Milky Way*, which won the Gival Press Poetry Award, a Silver Independent Publishers' Award, a Hoffer Award, and the Adirondack Center for Writing Poetry Award. She is the author of the chapbooks *Sequel* and *Neoclassical Barbra*, as well as *Haiku in English*. She has published poems in many journals such as *Rattle, Salmagundi,* and *The Nervous Breakdown.* A professor of English at The College of Saint Rose in Albany, New York, she directs their MFA program.

ABOUT THE ARTIST

Joseph Cornell (1903-1972), American assemblage artist, was best known for his "memory boxes" or "poetic theaters," in which he arranged old photos, Victorian bric-a-brac, dime-store trinkets, and ephemera from the used bookstores and thrift shops of New York City. He also made experimental films, and flat collages from the dossiers he kept on his obsessions, including ballerinas and actresses. Famously reclusive, he lived most of his life on Utopia Parkway in Flushing, Queens, caring for his mother and handicapped younger brother. Self-taught, Cornell became highly acclaimed, with work in museum collections worldwide. His last show was for children, with boxes displayed at child height, and refreshments of brownies and cherry soda.

ABOUT THE WORD WORKS

The Word Works, a nonprofit literary organization, publishes contemporary poetry and presents public programs.

The Hilary Tham Capital Collection presents work by poets who volunteer for literary nonprofit organizations. Nomination forms are requested from qualifying nonprofits by April 15 and manuscript submissions from nominated poets by May 1. Other imprints include the Washington Prize, International Editions, and The Tenth Gate Prize. A reading period is also held in May.

Monthly, The Word Works offers free literary programs in the Chevy Chase, MD, Café Muse series, and each summer, it holds free poetry programs in Washington, D.C.'s Rock Creek Park. Annually in June, two high school students debut in the Joaquin Miller Poetry Series as winners of the Jacklyn Potter Young Poets Competition. Since 1974, Word Works programs have included: "In the Shadow of the Capitol," a symposium and archival project on the African American intellectual community in segregated Washington, D.C.; the Gunston Arts Center Poetry Series; the Poet Editor panel discussions at The Writer's Center; and Master Class workshops.

As a 501(c)3 organization, The Word Works has received awards from the National Endowment for the Arts, the National Endowment for the Humanities, the D.C. Commission on the Arts & Humanities, the Witter Bynner Foundation, Poets & Writers, The Writer's Center, Bell Atlantic, the David G. Taft Foundation, and others, including many generous private patrons.

The Word Works has established an archive of artistic and administrative materials in the Washington Writing Archive housed in the George Washington University Gelman Library. It is a member of the Council of Literary Magazines and Presses and its books are distributed by Small Press Distribution.

FROM THE HILARY THAM CAPITAL COLLECTION

Mel Belin, *Flesh That Was Chrysalis*
Doris Brody, *Judging the Distance*
Sarah Browning, *Whiskey in the Garden of Eden*
Grace Cavalieri, *Pinecrest Rest Haven*
Christopher Conlon, *Gilbert and Garbo in Love*
  & *Mary Falls: Requiem for Mrs. Surratt*
Donna Denizé, *Broken like Job*
W. Perry Epes, *Nothing Happened*
Bernadette Geyer, *The Scabbard of Her Throat*
Barbara G. S. Hagerty, *Twinzilla*
James Hopkins, *Eight Pale Women*
Brandon Johnson, *Love's Skin*
Marilyn McCabe, *Perpetual Motion*
Judith McCombs, *The Habit of Fire*
James McEwen, *Snake Country*
Miles David Moore, *The Bears of Paris*
  & *Rollercoaster*
Kathi Morrison-Taylor, *By the Nest*
Michael Shaffner, *The Good Opinion of Squirrels*
Maria Terrone, *The Bodies We Were Loaned*
Hilary Tham, *Bad Names for Women*
  & *Counting*
Barbara Ungar, *Charlotte Brontë, You Ruined My Life*
Jonathan Vaile, *Blue Cowboy*
Tera Vale Ragan, *Reading the Ground*
Rosemary Winslow, *Green Bodies*
Michele Wolf, *Immersion*
Joseph Zealberg, *Covalence*

WASHINGTON PRIZE BOOKS

Nathalie F. Anderson, *Following Fred Astaire*, 1998
Michael Atkinson, *One Hundred Children Waiting for a Train*, 2001
Molly Bashaw, *The Whole Field Still Moving Inside It*, 2013
Carrie Bennett, *biography of water*, 2004
Peter Blair, *Last Heat*, 1999
John Bradley, *Love-in-Idleness: The Poetry of Roberto Zingarello*,
      1995, 2ND edition 2015
Richard Carr, *Ace*, 2008
Jamison Crabtree, *Rel[AM]ent*, 2014
B. K. Fischer, *St. Rage's Vault*, 2012
Ann Rae Jonas, *A Diamond Is Hard But Not Tough*, 1997
Frannie Lindsay, *Mayweed*, 2009
Richard Lyons, *Fleur Carnivore*, 2005
Fred Marchant, *Tipping Point*, 1993, 2ND edition 2013
Ron Mohring, *Survivable World*, 2003
Brad Richard, *Motion Studies*, 2010
Jay Rogoff, *The Cutoff*, 1994
Prartho Sereno, *Call from Paris*, 2007, 2ND edition 2013
Enid Shomer, *Stalking the Florida Panther*, 1987
John Surowiecki, *The Hat City after Men Stopped Wearing Hats*, 2006
Miles Waggener, *Phoenix Suites*, 2002
Mike White, *How to Make a Bird with Two Hands*, 2011
Nancy White, *Sun, Moon, Salt*, 1992, 2ND edition 2010

THE TENTH GATE PRIZE

Lisa Sewell, *Impossible Object*, 2014

INTERNATIONAL EDITIONS

Keyne Cheshire (trans.), *Murder at Jagged Rock: A Tragedy
    by Sophocles*
Yoko Danno & James C. Hopkins, *The Blue Door*
Moshe Dor, Barbara Goldberg, Giora Leshem, eds.,
    The Stones Remember: Native Israeli Poetry
Moshe Dor (Barbara Goldberg, trans.), *Scorched by the Sun*
Lee Sang (Myong-Hee Kim, trans.), *Crow's Eye View:
    The Infamy of Lee Sang, Korean Poet*
Vladimir Levchev (Henry Taylor, trans.), *Black Book of the
    Endangered Species*

OTHER WORD WORKS BOOKS

Karren L. Alenier, *Wandering on the Outside*
Karren L. Alenier, Hilary Tham, Miles David Moore, eds.,
    Winners: A Retrospective of the Washington Prize
Christopher Bursk, ed., *Cool Fire*
Barbara Goldberg, *Berta Broadfoot and Pepin the Short*
W.T. Pfefferle, *My Coolest Shirt*
Jacklyn Potter, Dwaine Rieves, Gary Stein, eds.,
    Cabin Fever: Poets at Joaquin Miller's Cabin
Robert Sargent, *Aspects of a Southern Story
    & A Woman from Memphis*

CPSIA information can be obtained at www.ICGtesting.com
Printed in the USA
BVOW01s0413270215

389177BV00002B/2/P